WHITE WOLVES

YEAR 5

Stories from Different Cultures

MARY GREEN

Teachers' Resource for Guided Reading

A & C Black • London

Contents

White Wolves Series Consultant: Sue Ellis, Centre for Literacy in Primary Education

Reprinted 2011
First published 2009 by
A & C Black Publishers Ltd
36 Soho Square, London, W1D 3QY
www.acblack.com

Text copyright © 2009 Mary Green
Illustrations copyright © 2009 Adam Larkum, Teresa Murfin, David Dean

The right of Mary Green to be identified as author and the rights of Adam Larkum, Teresa Murfin and David Dean to be identified as the illustrators of this work have been asserted by them in accordance with the Copyrights, Designs and Patents Act 1988.

ISBN 978-1-4081-1242-7
A CIP catalogue for this book is available from the British Library.

This book is produced using paper that is made from wood grown in managed, sustainable forests. It is natural, renewable and recyclable. The logging and manufacturing processes conform to the environmental regulations of the country of origin.

Printed in Great Britain by Martins the Printers, Berwick Upon Tweed.

Introduction

What is Guided Reading?

Guided Reading is a valuable part of literacy work within the classroom, bridging the gap between shared and independent reading. A teacher usually works with a small group of children, who are of similar reading abilities, using a text that has been carefully selected to match the reading ability of the group.

The group setting naturally leads to discussion about the book. The teacher's role is to support pupils in their reading and discussion, and encourage them to respond to the text in a variety of different ways, including personal response. In Guided Reading children can put into practice the reading strategies that have been taught during Shared Reading sessions, and the teacher can monitor their progress more closely.

Aims of Guided Reading

With careful organisation and selection of appropriate texts, Guided Reading can:
- improve reading fluency;
- inspire confidence and promote enjoyment of reading;
- deepen understanding of texts;
- provide an opportunity for purposeful discussion, both teacher-led and spontaneous;
- provide a context for focused talk and listening, including role-play and drama activities;
- offer a stimulus for independent writing;
- provide an opportunity for the teacher to monitor the progress of individual children.

The main aim of Guided Reading sessions is to help children become independent readers.

Assessment

Guided Reading is an excellent opportunity to observe and assess the reading strategies used by individual children. When listening to individual children reading aloud, check for accuracy, fluency and understanding, and note the strategies they use to make sense of less familiar words.

The photocopiable record card on p. 42 may be used to record your observations about individual pupils within each group, noting particular strengths and needs. These observations may be used to help note progression and inform your assessment of children's reading development.

Ongoing assessment will also help you to identify when Guided Reading groups need to be reorganised. Children progress at different rates; those who are progressing more rapidly may benefit from reading more challenging texts, while children who are struggling may need opportunities to read more supportive texts.

How to organise Guided Reading

Many teachers find it helpful to organise daily, dedicated Guided Reading sessions to ensure an uninterrupted focus on the group. It works well if each session has a teaching sequence, and the suggestions in this guide offer a structure that you can draw on to make the most of each text and the learning opportunities within them.

Ideally, each group should have a session of Guided Reading every week. Other children in the class can be engaged in a variety of purposeful, independent activities, such as working on an activity relating to a previous Guided Reading session, carrying out reading journals, or paired reading with books of their own choice.

How to Use This Book

Teaching sequences

This guide outlines five teaching sequences to support the use of three Year 5 books with a Guided Reading group:

Granny Ting Ting – to help less confident readers gain more independence

Ever Clever Eva – for independent readers

Bamba Beach – for more experienced readers.

The teaching sequences take into account important elements of reading at Year 5. However, they will need to be adapted to take into consideration the specific needs of individual children within a group to ensure engagement and progress.

The teaching sequences have been planned to be approximately 30 minutes in length, although this will vary depending on how many of the ideas for "Returning to the text" you choose to include.

Independent reading

Each Guided Reading session is likely to be a combination of silent reading, reading aloud and discussion about the text, with the emphasis on reading for meaning. It will be important to hear all children read aloud at some point during the session in order to monitor their progress. However, less-experienced readers will probably need to spend more time reading aloud each session as they are likely to require a higher level of support developing fluency.

Fluency and understanding are both important in reading. Modelling how to read a sentence, with appropriate phrasing and expression, may help children to make sense of the text. Guided Reading offers many opportunities for word and sentence level work, but any significant difficulties demonstrated by individual children should be noted on the record card on p. 42 and addressed afterwards so as not to inhibit the group's understanding and enjoyment of the story.

Returning to the text

The questions and prompts in this section may be used to elicit children's understanding of the text. The questions can be asked either during reading or at the end of the chapter. It is not necessary to ask all the questions, as many of these will be covered in discussion arising spontaneously from reading the text. Encourage children to find the relevant parts of the text to support their answers and ask them to give reasons when offering opinions.

Experienced readers require less "literal" questioning and should be encouraged to develop higher order reading skills, for example prediction, inference and deduction.

Additional ideas for exploring the text further include:

- identifying features such as alliteration, similes, compound words, use of italics and capitalisation;
- opportunities for developing prediction skills;
- a range of role-play and drama activities;
- a stimulus for the activity sheet that follows.

It is important that groups have the experience of a reflective conversation about the book and not a "twenty questions" approach to test comprehension.

Next steps

The activity sheets may be used for independent work either in school or as homework. They offer a variety of ways for children to demonstrate their understanding of the stories, along with valuable opportunities for writing for different purposes.

Target Statements for Reading

The NLS target statements for reading at Year 5 will help inform your planning for progression in reading.

Word recognition and phonic knowledge:
- use knowledge of words, roots, derivations and spelling patterns to read unknown words.

Grammatical awareness:
- understand how complex sentences are constructed and punctuated and use this to deepen understanding when reading.

Use of context:
- understand how stories may vary, e.g. in pace, build up, sequence, complication and resolution.

Knowing how texts work:
- identify features of different fiction genres, e.g. science fiction, adventure, myths and legends.

Interpretations and response: literary text:
- identify the point of view from which a story is told and respond to this, e.g. by retelling from a different point of view.
- understand the difference between literal and figurative language, e.g. by discussing the effects of imagery in poetry and prose.
- recognise how characters are presented in different ways and respond to this with reference to the text.
- infer meaning with reference to the text but also applying wider experience, e.g. why a character is behaving in a particular way.

Attitude:
- develop an active response to own reading, e.g. by empathising with characters, imagining events.
- use the blurb, front cover, reviews, etc. to make informed decisions about which books to read.
- take part in peer group discussions and be prepared to widen reading experience based on recommendation.

Granny Ting Ting
by *Patrice Lawrence*

About the book

Shayla and her mother live in Trinidad and are staying with Shayla's granny while she recovers from an eye operation. The family are waiting for Shayla's cousin Michael and his mother Jess to arrive from London. It has been four years since they visited Trinidad and Shayla remembers how well she and Michael got on. However, when they arrive, Michael seems to have grown into a moody teenager. The present of an electronic "pet" that he brings for Shayla from London seems to illustrate the difference between their urban and rural lives. Rather than spend time with Shayla and Granny, Michael borrows the rusty old bike that Granny used on her wedding day, but she is happy to see someone else on it, as she can't ride.

The relationship between Shayla and Michael is tested as a rivalry develops. Michael is encouraged to try hot pepper sauce, and he rises to the challenge with nasty consequences. They both climb Shayla's favourite lime tree, but Michael outwits the over-confident Shayla. Even when they tell ghost stories, the teasing continues. Michael's story includes a trick played on Shayla. This causes great amusement to everyone else and Michael is acknowledged as being a true member

of his Trinidadian family.

Michael tells Shayla how exciting London is and Shayla begins to feel Trinidad is wanting. Nonetheless they take a trip to the beach through beautiful landscape and see cormorants diving and places where turtles lay their eggs. By the next day however, Shayla is sad. The electronic pet holds no appeal and Michael seems to be more accomplished at everything. After confiding in Granny however, she feels reassured and devises a clever plan. When Michael and Aunty Jess return from visiting relatives, they see Granny wobbling down the road on the old bike. The whole family are amazed. Shayla has succeeded in teaching Granny to ride, something no one else has been able to do. Michael is impressed, and the story comes to a close as the two cousins agree a truce and to have fun together from then on.

But it was.

There, wobbling down the road towards them on Grandpa's rusty old bicycle, was...

"Granny!" Michael's voice was full of admiration. She juddered to a stop

in front of them. "Mum told me you couldn't ride that bike!"

Granny winked at Shayla. "I had an excellent teacher."

Aunty Jess held the bike so Granny could get off. "But I tried to teach you and you pedalled backwards!"

"And then you landed in a bush," Mommy added.

"My father tried, and your grandpa. And even Uncle William." Granny beamed. "But only Shayla has managed to succeed."

74

75

Granny Ting Ting: Teaching Sequence 1

Summary of Chapter One

Ten-year-old Shayla lives in Arouca, Trinidad. She is waiting impatiently for the arrival of her cousin Michael and her aunty Jess from London. The last time they visited Trinidad was four years ago, but Shayla remembers how well she and Michael played together. When at last they arrive, Shayla is overcome with shyness. While the adults enthusiastically greet each other, she sees Michael, older and aloof, propped against the car in his baggy jeans and baseball cap.

Teaching Sequence

Introduction
- Discuss the front cover and read the blurb. What is the story about and where is it set?
- Point to Trinidad on a map. Mention that it is part of the Caribbean islands.

Independent reading
Ask the children to read Chapter One. Emphasise reading for meaning.
- Discuss the meaning of unfamiliar or difficult words and phrases: *recently, operation, Arouca, Trinidad, bamboo* (p. 8), *fireflies, papaya, cicadas, screeched* (p. 10), *approaching* (p. 11), *urged, dreadlocks* (p. 12), *shadowy* (p. 13), *grasshopper, instantly* (p. 14), *approve, hint of mischief* (p. 15), *grumpy phase, steered* (p. 17), *sliding door* (p. 18).
- Refer to compound words and the use of the hyphen: *Ten-year-old* (p. 7), *hide-and-seek* (p. 8), *T-shirt* (p. 16).
- Discuss the way the writer produces the sound of the cicadas: "Queetch, queek, queal" (p. 10). Ask the children to say it aloud.

Returning to the text
Build on children's understanding by asking questions during reading or when the chapter is finished. Encourage them to point to evidence in the story to support their answers.

1) How can you tell Shayla is impatient and excited? (She keeps asking when Michael and Aunty Jess will arrive and can't wait to see Michael again (pp. 7, 8 and 11).)
2) What do you think Shayla expects Michael to be like four years on? (She doesn't think he will have changed (pp. 8–9).)
3) What are the cicadas doing and how do they do it? (They are performing mating calls, by exercising the flaps on their abdomens to create noise (p. 10).)
4) How do you think Shayla and Michael feel when they see each other again? (Shayla is shy and surprised (pp. 12 and 14), Michael is restrained and moody (pp. 16 –17).)

Discuss the rural setting depicted through strong imagery: "the fireflies' shining green bottoms bump together under the papaya tree", "the cicadas screeched their night song" (p. 10), and through the simile: "She's been bouncing around like a grasshopper" (p. 14). Point out that the typical wildlife and vegetation places the story firmly in the Caribbean. Contrast Michael's urban demeanour and attitude (pp. 16 –17) with the unfamiliar environment in which he finds himself.

In pairs, ask the children to carry out a role-play activity based around the meeting between Shayla and Michael. Remind them of their answers to questions 1, 2 and 4 above, then give the children a few minutes to reread pp. 15–17 and explore the emotions the different characters felt.

Next steps
Refer to Activity Sheet 1: "Opposites", in which the children explore the differences between the characters of Shayla and Michael, and offer advice about how they can get along.

Opposites

In what ways are Shayla and Michael different? Write four more points in the boxes about each character. Then add some sentences giving advice about how they could get along with each other.

Shayla	
	● Lives in the countryside ● _____ ● _____ ● _____ ● _____

Michael	
	● Lives in the city ● _____ ● _____ ● _____ ● _____

_____

_____

_____

_____

White Wolves Teachers' Resource
for Guided Reading Year 5
Stories from Different Cultures
© A & C Black 2009

Granny Ting Ting: Teaching Sequence 2

Summary of Chapter Two

Michael, having recovered from jet lag, gives Shayla a gift from London, a fashionable electronic "pet". However, when Aunty Jess and Shayla's mother go off, Michael is reluctant to spend time alone with Granny and Shayla. From the storage space under the house, he pulls out a rusty old bike and rides away. Shayla is alarmed, but Granny is unconcerned and tells Shayla the story of the old bike. It was the one that she and Grandpa used at their wedding, since at that time no one owned a car, and she is happy to see someone ride it again.

Teaching Sequence

Introduction
- Ask the children to describe the characters and recount the main events that took place in Chapter One.

Independent reading
Ask the children to read Chapter Two. Emphasise reading for meaning.
- Discuss the meaning of unfamiliar or difficult words: *clatter* (p. 19), *university, stilts, rusting* (p. 20), *Trinidad time, tamarind balls* (p. 21), *powderpuff tree, hummingbird* (p. 22), *mango tree, lime tree* (p. 23), *rummaged, peered* (p. 24), *tackle, gossip* (p. 26), *lizard* (p. 27), *stomped* (p. 28), *clomped* (p. 29), *horse and cart, side-saddle, crossbar, potholes* (p. 31), *embarrassed* (p. 33).

Returning to the text
Build on children's understanding by asking questions during reading or when the chapter is finished. Encourage them to point to evidence in the story to support their answers.
1) What is Shayla's attitude to Michael at the beginning of this chapter? (She is still curious about him and assumes he will want her company (pp. 20–21).)

2) What do you think Shayla feels about Michael's present? (The children should infer Shayla's lack of enthusiasm for the present, from the statement: "The thing beeped at Shayla. She put it down on the table." (p. 25).)
3) What do you think of the way Michael behaves when he rides away? Would you have done the same? (Encourage the children to view Michael's behaviour from both his point of view and Shayla's, taking into account his desire to appear grown-up and Shayla's desire to be hospitable (p. 28).)

Discuss Shayla's feelings about Granny's back yard. Point to evidence in the text to describe what she sees: the "powderpuff tree", the "jewel-coloured hummingbird" (p. 22), her "favourite lime tree" (p. 23). The children should also speculate how she feels when she is there.

Ask the children to consider how the relationship between Michael and Shayla will develop. Will they quarrel, remain distant or become friends? The children could share any similar experiences they have had.

Discuss what we learn about Granny in this chapter. Why does she keep the old bike? (She keeps the bike because it reminds her of Grandpa (p. 30).) Why does she tell stories about the past? (She likes to recall bitter-sweet memories (p. 31).) What is her attitude to Michael taking the bike? (She adopts a relaxed attitude (p. 30).) Help the children to explore what we learn about Granny's character from the questions raised.

Next steps
Refer to Activity Sheet 2: "Electronic Pet", in which the children design an electronic pet. Encourage them to use the imperative when they write the instructions. An example is given.

Electronic Pet

Michael gives Shayla an electronic pet. It has buttons that she must press to feed it or take it for a walk. Design your own electronic pet and label what the different buttons do. Decide:

- what it will look like
- what functions it can perform and the noises it makes
- how it works.

Underneath your design, write instructions explaining how to use it. Remember to give your pet a name.

Instructions:

- Press —————————————————————————

- ————————————————————————————

- ————————————————————————————

- ————————————————————————————

- ————————————————————————————

White Wolves Teachers' Resource
for Guided Reading Year 5
Stories from Different Cultures
© A & C Black 2009

Summary of Chapter Three

Shayla and Michael help Granny make tamarind balls. Shayla, aware that tamarinds are hot, suggests that Michael should eat the pulp and wash it down with ginger beer. He rises to the challenge. The competition escalates to the point when Michael tries fiery pepper sauce. When he finally recovers, Granny shows Michael her trees, including Shayla's favourite lime tree. Michael and Shayla compete to see who can climb higher. Shayla, having climbed the tree many times, is confident she can win, but when she sees a menacing, brightly coloured caterpillar she comes down the tree as quickly as she can.

Teaching Sequence

Introduction
Ask the children to select three things they have learned in Chapter Two and share them with the group.

Independent reading
Ask the children to read Chapter Two. Emphasise reading for meaning.

- Discuss the meaning of unfamiliar or difficult words: *sourness* (p. 35), *Nigeria, pulp* (p. 36), *ginger beer, massive* (p. 38), *glared, spiciest* (p. 39), *mush, wrenched, plunged, fumes, wafted* (p. 40), *soldier ants, gargling* (p. 41), *amusement, bold* (p. 42), *sugar cane, cashew, stinking toe* (p.43), *shrugged, grasped, foothold, heaved* (p. 45), *scrambling* (p. 46), *adventure playground* (p. 48).
- Draw attention to the use of single words to create tension, when Michael tries the pepper sauce: *Silence. Shock.* (p. 40).

Returning to the text
Build on children's understanding by asking questions during reading or when the chapter is finished. Encourage them to point to evidence in the story to support their answers.

1) What are tamarind balls and why does Shayla love them? (They are brown, sugary sweets. Shayla loves their combination of sweetness and sourness (p. 35).)
2) What does Shayla encourage Michael to do with the tamarind pulp and the ginger beer? Why? (She encourages Michael to combine the two to cause him discomfort. Tarmind pulp is sour and combined with ginger beer becomes spicy (pp. 37–38).)
3) Why do you think Michael ignores Granny's advice not to touch the hot pepper sauce? (He rises to Shayla's provocation in an attempt to prove his fearlessness (p. 40).)
4) In what way does Michael outwit Shayla, and how? (He is more successful at climbing the lime tree. Shayla is put off when she sees a caterpillar (pp. 43–48).)

Discuss what Granny thinks of the exchanges between Shayla and Michael. Is she annoyed, irritated or amused? The children could consider the way she speaks to Shayla (pp. 37–38). Ask the children if they think Michael should have allowed himself to be provoked. What would they have done in the same circumstances? Also ask the children *why* Shayla is provoking Michael.

Draw attention to the use of metaphor: "A hundred soldier ants were biting his tongue" (p. 41) and simile: "It looked like a small giant was dangling his feet through the branches" (p. 43). Discuss the difference between the two. Point out that they are both images (or pictures in the mind that appeal to our senses.)

Next steps
The children can complete Activity Sheet 3: "Similes", in which they are asked to create similes for six things mentioned in Chapter Three.

Similes

Remember that a simile compares one thing with another using the linking words "like" or "as". For example: "The bike clattered along *like* a supermarket trolley that had lost a wheel" or "The bike was *as* rusty *as* an old tin can thrown on a rubbish heap".

Make up your own similes for the following:

- Shayla's favourite lime tree... ———————————

  ————————————————————————

  ————————————————————————

- Granny's cocoa tree... ———————————

  ————————————————————————

  ————————————————————————

- The tamarind... ———————————

  ————————————————————————

  ————————————————————————

- The ginger beer... ———————————

  ————————————————————————

  ————————————————————————

- Granny's ice cream... ———————————

  ————————————————————————

  ————————————————————————

- The black-and-yellow caterpillar... ———————————

  ————————————————————————

  ————————————————————————

White Wolves Teachers' Resource
for Guided Reading Year 5
Stories from Different Cultures
© A & C Black 2009

Granny Ting Ting: Teaching Sequence 4

Summary of Chapter Four

There is a power cut, so Granny tells the ghost story of Uncle William, who meets a douenne, a ghost child. Tradition has it that a douenne may lure a child away and so Uncle William picks up the douenne and returns it to the woods. Michael follows Granny's tale with the story of his meeting with a hooded skeleton who drops something slimy into his hands – eyeballs! Michael has placed some peeled chennets into the bag of tamarind balls, and at the appropriate point Shayla unwittingly squeezes them. The family collapse in laughter and Michael has become what Granny calls "a real Trinidadian".

Teaching Sequence

Introduction
Ask the children to sum up the relationship between Shayla and Michael in Chapter Three.

Independent reading
Ask the children to read Chapter Four. Emphasise reading for meaning.

- Discuss the meaning of unfamiliar or difficult words: *mummy* (p. 49), *soap operas, mosquito* (p. 50), *power cut* (p. 51), *imagination* (p. 52), *rooster, whimper* (p. 53), *fluttered, cone-shaped, restless* (p. 55), *ignored, lure* (p. 56), *staggered* (p. 57), *statues, tombs, ivy, headstone* (p. 59), *chennets, Trinidadian, triumphantly* (p. 62).
- Ensure the children grasp that a *douenne* (p. 54) is a ghost child and *Du Shayne* (p. 58) is a ghostly skeleton.

Returning to the text
Build on children's understanding by asking questions during reading or when the chapter is finished. Encourage them to point to evidence in the story to support their answers.

1) What time of day is it and what are the family doing as the chapter opens? (It is evening and the family are watching a soap opera (pp. 49–50).)
2) Why are the family so amused by Michael's story? (He plays a joke on Shayla, who thinks the chennets in the bag are Du Shayne's eyeballs and screams (p. 61).)
3) Granny comments to Michael: "You tell stories like a real Trinidadian" (p. 62). What does she mean? (Michael has told the ghost story engagingly, as they do in Trinidad. It's also a way of saying that Michael may be a Londoner, but he's also a Trinidadian.)

Discuss the different ghosts depicted in the story, explaining that these are part of Trinidadian or Caribbean folklore. Both stories are presented as being true. Ask the children if they think the stories really are true and whether or not a story that is true has more impact than one that isn't.

Explore what makes the stories successful, pointing to the way surprise and tension are created. For example, at the point where the rooster crows in the story told by Granny, Shayla calls, "Cocker doodle-doo!" causing surprise. Ask the children how Michael responds to Shayla ("in a shaky voice" (p. 53)). Point to how pauses create tension, either by the use of full stops or dashes ("…it came again. A whimper." (p. 53) "…it was – a douenne" (p. 55)). Ask the children to read the appropriate sentences with expression. The children can work in pairs to locate similar examples of surprise and tension in the story Michael tells (pp. 60–61).

Next steps
Refer to Activity Sheet 4: "Things That Go Bump in the Night", in which the children make notes for a ghost story. Remind them that they do not have to write the story, only tell it.

Things That Go Bump in the Night

Both Granny and Michael tell ghost stories. Make up one of your own. Write notes about what you will include in the boxes below, then tell your story to a partner. Remember you can always change or add to your story as you tell it.

Where will the story take place?

- _____
- _____
- _____
- _____

Who will the characters be? (Think of two or three.)

- _____
- _____
- _____

What will happen?

- _____
- _____
- _____

How will the story end?

- _____
- _____
- _____

White Wolves Teachers' Resource
for Guided Reading Year 5
Stories from Different Cultures
© A & C Black 2009

Granny Ting Ting: Teaching Sequence 5

Summary of Chapter Five

Michael tells Shayla all the exciting things he can do in London. Shayla points out that in Trinidad they have the beach, which they are about to visit. The next day, after trying to play with her electronic pet, Shayla confides to Granny that she feels inferior to Michael. Granny reassures her, and when Michael and Aunty Jess visit a relative Shayla devises a plan. When everyone comes back, Granny is wobbling down the road on her old bike. Over the years, everyone has tried to teach Granny to ride it, but only Shayla has succeeded. Michael congratulates her, admitting he couldn't have done it and offers a truce to their rivalry.

Teaching Sequence

Introduction
Ask the children to sum up the events of the story so far and ask them how they think it will end.

Independent reading
Ask the children to read Chapter Five. Emphasise reading for meaning.
- Discuss the meaning of unfamiliar or difficult words: *trumpeting, conch shell* (p. 63), *pod* (p. 64), *waterfalls, weaver-bird, wrinkly* (p. 65), *cormorants, swooped, river pool, tadpoles* (p. 66), *sand dunes, turtles* (p. 67), *marching ants, iguanas* (p. 69), *Tante, squinted* (p. 72), *admiration, juddered* (p. 74), *hot-headed* (p. 76).

Returning to the text
Build on children's understanding by asking questions during reading or when the chapter is finished. Encourage them to point to evidence in the story to support their answers.
1) What do Michael and Shayla talk about in the lime tree? (The exciting things you can do in London (pp. 64–65).)
2) What creatures do the children see at the beach and the river pool? (Cormorants diving for fish (p. 66), tadpoles, crab holes (p. 67).
3) What does Shayla think of her electronic pet? Why is she troubled by it? (Shayla thinks it isn't as interesting as ants or iguanas and is troubled because she feels she is out of step with the girls in London (p. 69).)

Explore Shayla's conflicting feelings about Trinidad, her home and the attractions London has to offer. Ask the children why she feels inferior to Michael. Is she right to feel like this? If they were Granny, what advice would they give Shayla?

Reread pp. 65–67, paying special attention to the images depicted of Trinidad. Can the children visualise the steep roads and waterfalls and the beauty of the scenery? What do the children imagine "the wrinkly sea" refers to? (p. 65). Ask them what part of the day out they would enjoy most. (For example, watching cormorants dive, finding tadpoles or crab holes.) What trips to the seaside have the children been on? Ask them to share their experiences.

Discuss the ending of the story. Were the children surprised that Shayla taught Granny to ride the bike? What skills would Shayla need that Michael and the grown-ups didn't have? (For example, patience and the ability to give support while also encouraging Granny to ride on her own.) Also discuss the rivalry between Shayla and Michael. Who is the real winner, as mentioned in the blurb on the back of the book? Are they both winners? What do the cousins mean when they say "truce"?

Next steps
Refer to Activity Sheet 5: "Trinidad Diary", in which, as Shayla, the children write a series of diary entries about Michael's visit to Trinidad and how she feels about their relationship.

Trinidad Diary

Imagine you are Shayla. Write a series of diary entries about Michael's visit to Granny's house and how she feels about him.

When I first saw Michael I couldn't _____

_____

_____

_____

_____

Michael thinks he's so clever, so this morning _____

_____

_____

_____

_____

I have been happy and sad today. I asked Granny why Michael _____

_____

_____

_____

_____

White Wolves Teachers' Resource
for Guided Reading Year 5
Stories from Different Cultures
© A & C Black 2009

Ever Clever Eva
by *Andrew Fusek Peters*

About the book

Eva's father, Eduard, is poor so she works for her rich uncle, Jan, but the miserly Jan refuses to pay Eva the cow he has promised when it is fully grown. So Eduard takes Jan to court, where the brothers are given three riddles to answer on the following day. Eduard answers correctly and the judge awards him the cow. However, he discovers that Eva has helped Eduard and presents him with a series of difficult tasks for his daughter, which Eva duly carries out. The judge, impressed by Eva's beauty and intelligence, asks her to marry him. She accepts, with the condition that she will never interfere in the judge's work.

A year later, Eva meets a poor man who has lost a court case, as the judge has taken a bribe. Eva sets the man a task to trick the judge into granting justice. The judge discovers what Eva has done and banishes her for breaking her word, but allows one concession: she can take whatever is dearest to her. Eva devises a plan. She tells the judge the tale of the woman who becomes a wealthy doctor, through Death's help. When Death places himself at the head of the bed the patient immediately recovers. One day the woman is summoned to cure the king's son. If she succeeds she can marry him, otherwise she will die. But Death has placed

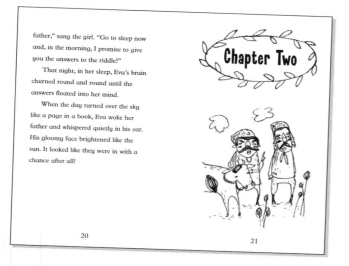

himself at the foot of the prince's bed, so he cannot recover. The woman uses her wits, turns the bed around and cures the prince. They marry amidst great rejoicing. Then Death intervenes, snatches the woman and takes her to a room where millions of oil lamps flicker, one for each life. The woman's lamp is so low that she will soon die. So she tells Death a story. He falls asleep and the woman replenishes her lamp and the prince's, and escapes.

By now Eva's own husband, the judge, is snoring. She asks the servants to put him to bed and take the bed to her father's cottage. When the judge wakes, Eva tells him that she has left his house, as he wished, taking the dearest thing with her – himself. The judge softens, forgives Eva and as a reward for her cleverness makes her the new judge of the city.

Ever Clever Eva: Teaching Sequence 1

Summary of Chapter One

Eva's father, Eduard, is poor, so at the age of 14 Eva goes to work as a goose girl for her rich uncle, Master Jan. Instead of pay, Eva receives the promise of a young calf when it has grown. But Jan goes back on his promise and Eva angrily returns to her father, who marches Jan to the court in Prague. Unable to work out who is telling the truth, the judge presents the brothers with three riddles to be answered the following day.

Teaching Sequence

Introduction
Discuss the front cover and read the blurb. Refer to the "Author's Note" and discuss the origins of the tale and the changes made by the author. Find Prague on a world map. Explain the Czech Republic used to be known as Czechoslovakia.

Independent reading
Ask the children to read Chapter One. Emphasise reading for meaning.
- Discuss the meaning of unfamiliar or difficult words and names: *Prague* (p. 9), *cackling, brass* (p. 10), *keeled* (p. 13), *cunningly innocent, hay barn, scavenge* (p. 14), *fuming* (p. 15), *scoundrel, courthouse, judge* (p. 16), *dumpling* (p. 18), *churned* (p. 20).

Returning to the text
Build on children's understanding by asking questions during reading or when the chapter is finished. Encourage them to point to evidence in the story to support their answers.
1) How does Master Jan treat Eva? What does he promise her? (He is unkind and works her hard. He promises a calf when it is grown (p. 12).)
2) Why does Eva return to her father in a rage? (Master Jan has broken his promise (p. 15).)
3) What does the judge decide to do and why?

(He presents Eduard and Jan with three riddles to solve. Whoever gives the correct answer will win the cow (p. 18).)

Draw attention to the features of the folk-tale setting: the traditional opening, "Long, long ago…" (p. 7); the rural occupations and references, such as goose girl, farm (pp. 9–10), calf, market (p. 12); how characters are sometimes addressed in the traditional way, "Master Jan" (p. 9).

Idioms are often used comically and suit the story's colloquial style. Draw attention to one or two and ask the children what they mean. For example: "bite the fingers that feed them" (p. 10), "with a spring in her step" (p. 12). The children can work in pairs to find other examples.

Refer to the numerous similes, such as: "as rich as a treasure box" (p. 9), "when the day turned over the sky like a page in a book" (p. 20). Ask the children to close their eyes and visualise the pictures that the author has created.

Discuss what the children have learned about Eva in Chapter One, distinguishing between fact and opinion. (For example, we know that Eva works as a goose girl. However, we can deduce that she works hard because she gets up at dawn and has many other jobs to do.)

Ask the children to try to answer the riddles the judge has set. They can work in pairs to think of more than one answer to each riddle.

Next steps
Ask the children to complete Activity Sheet 1: "Eva", in which they assemble a fact file and opinions about Eva's character. Remind them that they will need to separate facts about Eva from what they deduce about her (their opinions).

Eva

What have you learned about Eva in Chapter One? Complete the fact file below and make notes about Eva's character. Support your answers with examples from the text.

Eva Fact File	
Age: (beginning of the chapter)	
(end of the chapter)	
Where she lives	
Who she lives with	
Who she works for	
Her main job	
How Eva will be paid and when	

What is Eva like?

- hard working – she does many jobs. She gets up at dawn, cleans, washes clothes and cooks for Master Jan, as well as doing her main job.

- _____

  _____

- _____

  _____

- _____

  _____

- _____

  _____

White Wolves Teachers' Resource
for Guided Reading Year 5
Stories from Different Cultures
© A & C Black 2009

Ever Clever Eva: Teaching Sequence 2

Summary of Chapter Two

The brothers attend the courthouse to answer the riddles and on hearing their replies the judge awards the cow to Eduard. But he is suspicious and Eduard has to admit that Eva helped him with the answers. When the judge learns how beautiful Eva is, he presents Eduard with another riddle, a series of puzzles that Eva must solve. She meets all the conditions and, impressed by her intelligence as well as her beauty, the judge offers his hand in marriage and Eva accepts. However, she must make a promise: never to interfere in his work.

Teaching Sequence

Introduction
Recap on Chapter One, asking the children to name the characters introduced and recall three events.

Independent reading
Ask the children to read Chapter Two. Emphasise reading for meaning.
- Discuss the meaning of unfamiliar or difficult words: *taunts* (p. 23), *inhabitant, walkover* (p. 24), *justice* (p. 25), *case, appeals* (p. 26), *lock-up* (p. 27), *gong, shod, unshod, pasture* (p. 29), *ravishing, summoned* (p. 30), *ambled, cobbled, twilight* (p. 32), *decisive, moony* (p. 34).
- Discuss the meaning of the idioms: *made his head spin* (p. 29), *met his match* (p. 31).

Returning to the text
Build on children's understanding by asking questions during reading or when the chapter is finished. Encourage them to point to evidence in the story to support their answers.
1) Who answers the riddles correctly and why are we pleased? (Eduard answers correctly (p. 26). Master Jan is the villain who has tried to cheat Eva and lost.)
2) Why does the judge want to meet Eva? (He already know she is intelligent. When Eduard describes her beauty, it makes him interested in finding out more (p. 28).)
3) Why does the judge want to marry Eva? (She is clever and beautiful.)
4) Why might there be problems in the marriage for Eva? (She will not be content to ignore what the judge does (p. 35).)

Refer to the first set of riddles and take the children through them again, ensuring they grasp that both sets of answers are actually correct (pp. 25–26). Ask why they think the judge has chosen Eva's answers and awarded the case to Eduard. Encourage them to see how the answers given by Master Jan and his wife reflect their own private concerns and mercenary natures, while Eva's answers show a broader view of life.

The children can work in groups of three, to role-play the events in the court. Ask the class how the characters in the courthouse would be played: the judge, officious and powerful; Master Jan self-assured, then shocked and angry; Eduard, nervous and relieved, then perplexed. Encourage the children to memorise the answers to the riddles.

Discuss why Eva agrees to marry the judge. Does she love him? Explain that in the past women were less likely to marry for love. Marrying well meant marrying prosperously, since women had few rights and were reliant on marriage to secure their futures. Eva, being poor but clever, seizes her opportunity.

Next steps
Refer to Activity Sheet 2: "Riddle-mee-ree", in which the children are asked to create their own riddles using the model given. They can use rhyme or not as they please.

Riddle-mee-ree

Read the riddle below and try to guess the answer (which you can find at the bottom of the page).

I can ripple and trickle,
And curl up small,
Or climb giant heights,
And crashing, fall.

What am I?

Use the same idea to make your own riddles and give them to a partner to answer. You could think of your own topic, or choose from the following, which come from *Eva Clever Eva*:

A cow

_____

_____

_____

_____

What am I?

A goose

_____

_____

_____

_____

What am I?

Honey

_____

_____

_____

_____

What am I?

Gold

_____

_____

_____

_____

What am I?

Answer: A wave

White Wolves Teachers' Resource
for Guided Reading Year 5
Stories from Different Cultures
© A & C Black 2009

Ever Clever Eva: Teaching Sequence 3

Summary of Chapter Three

Eva meets an unhappy man in the market. His mare has born a foal, but his rich brother has claimed it for himself. The judge has ruled in favour of the brother and he suspects him of taking a bribe. Eva realises that the judge is her husband and that he has behaved foolishly, so she sets the man a task to trap the judge. When the judge discovers that Eva is involved, he banishes her from the house, but as a gesture of goodwill, he allows her to take the thing most dear to her.

Teaching Sequence

Introduction
Recap on Chapter Two, asking the children to explain how Eva's life has changed and why.

Independent reading
Ask the children to read Chapter Three. Emphasise reading for meaning.

- Discuss the meaning of unfamiliar or difficult words and phrases: *briefest glimmer of a smile* (p. 39), *woe, mare, stallion, foal, circumstances* (p. 40), *contribute, bribe* (p. 41), *wailed, snivelling* (p. 42), *rational, fellow* (p. 43), *consequences* (p. 47), *sprout, gesture of goodwill* (p. 48).

Returning to the text
Build on children's understanding by asking questions during reading or when the chapter is finished. Encourage them to point to evidence in the story to support their answers.

1) Who does Eva meet in the market place? (She meets a poor man with a story about how the judge accepted a bribe and made a bad decision in court (p. 41).)

2) What does Eva think of the judge's decision to award the man's brother the foal? (She thinks her husband is a fool (p. 41).)

3) What does Eva tell the man to do and why?

(The man is to appear to be fishing in grass and when the curious judge asks why, he is to say that he is "not as mad as he who believes that a stallion can give birth to a foal!" (p. 43). The judge will be forced to return the foal and justice will be served.)

Discuss whether or not Eva was right to break her promise. Ask the children to work in groups to talk about the following: What does Eva mean when she says: "Surely justice is more important than a mere word?". Do they agree or not? How would they have acted in Eva's place? Would they have told the judge what they had done, or kept it to themselves?

Ask the children to note how the man in the market place addresses Eva as "my lady" (p. 40). Also point out Eva's comment to him when he continues to complain: "Oh, stop snivelling!" (p. 42). What do they tell us about Eva? (The man's address tells us that he assumes Eva has a position of status. Eva's comment suggests that she has little time for self-pity.)

Reread p. 41 and draw attention to the author's choice of verbs showing Eva's impatience and alarm: *interrupted, shocked, demanded.*

Ask the children to reread pp. 46–48 and find examples of verbs that reveal the judge's temper. (*threatened, kicked, shouted, pointed, stomped, slammed*). What does this tell us about him? Discuss with the children whether or not the judge's behaviour is justified, taking into account that he has accepted a bribe.

Next steps
Refer to Activity Sheet 3: "Making Judgements", in which the children draw up a list of the judge's good and bad points and decide on the overall nature of his character.

Making Judgements

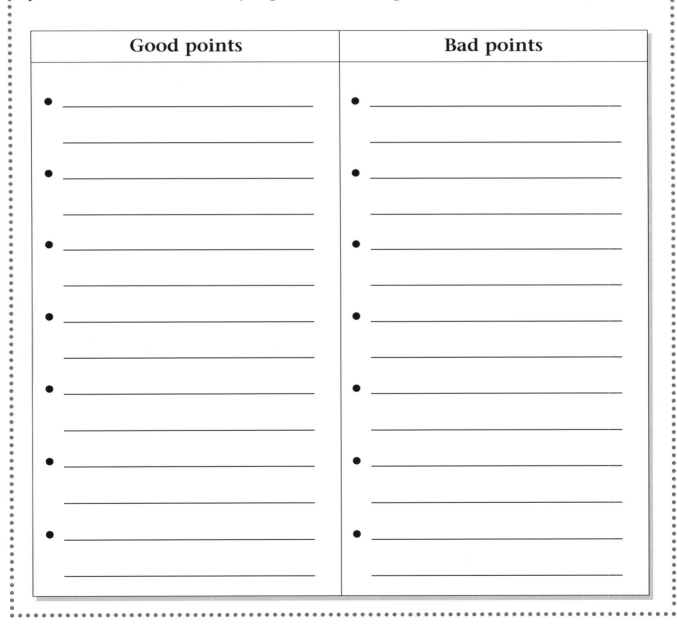

Think about the actions of the judge in the first three chapters. Then draw up a list of his good points and bad points, taking into account his treatment:

- of Eva
- of Eduard and Master Jan
- of the man Eva meets in the market place

Compare your list with a partner's and between you decide whether the judge is overall a good man or a bad one.

Good points	Bad points
● _____ _____	● _____ _____
● _____ _____	● _____ _____
● _____ _____	● _____ _____
● _____ _____	● _____ _____
● _____ _____	● _____ _____
● _____ _____	● _____ _____
● _____ _____	● _____ _____

White Wolves Teachers' Resource
for Guided Reading Year 5
Stories from Different Cultures
© A & C Black 2009

Ever Clever Eva: Teaching Sequence 4

Summary of Chapter Four

Eva devises a plan. She prepares the judge's favourite meal, and tells him the story about a woman and Death. One day Death calls at the woman's door and tells her that if she takes his advice she can become a successful doctor. Whenever Death stands at the head of the patient's bed, she is to place her hand on the patient's forehead and the patient will recover. But if Death should stand at the foot of the bed, the patient will die. The woman cures a poor young man and a rich wife and soon gains a reputation as a miracle worker. Then one day she is summoned to the king, whose son is ill. If she can save him, she can marry the young man. If not, she will be beheaded.

Teaching Sequence

Introduction
Recap on Chapter Three and ask the children what they think will happen to Eva.

Independent reading
Ask the children to read Chapter Four. Emphasise reading for meaning.

- Discuss the meaning of unfamiliar or difficult words and phrases: *sorrowful* (p. 51), *scurried*, *wafted* (p. 52), *tureens* (p. 53), *paprika, caraway, Czech* (p. 54), *stoked, innocently* (p. 55), *intention* (p. 56), *gloomy* (p. 57), *calling cards* (p. 58), *strewn* (p. 60), *Chinese whispers* (p. 61), *ember* (p. 62).

Returning to the text
Build on children's understanding by asking questions during reading or when the chapter is finished. Encourage them to point to evidence in the story to support their answers.

1) What does Eva's plan involve? (She cooks her husband's favourite meal and tells him a story, so he will fall asleep (pp. 52, 55 and 56).)

2) What meal do Eva and her husband eat and where does the recipe come from? (They eat pork in cream and paprika sauce, with caraway seed dumplings. It is a Czech recipe (p. 54).)

3) How does Death help the woman become rich? (By standing at the head of the bed, Death allows the patients to recover. (p. 58).)

4) If Death is not at the head of the bed, where is he and what happens to the patient? (Death is at the foot of the bed, and the patient dies (p. 58).)

Refer to the use of italics and ask the children why they think the author has used them. Ensure that the children distinguish between the story, *Ever Clever Eva*, and the story of the woman and Death that Eva tells. Discuss how the tale of the woman and Death is a story within a story.

Point to the use of capitals for emphasis (p. 63). Ask the children what they think their purpose is.

Carry out a thought-tracking exercise, in which you ask the children to express a character's thoughts and feelings. For example, select a child, naming them as a character (in this case Eva) and ask, "How did you feel when the judge agreed that you could cook a meal for him?" The child should answer instantly and in role.

Refer to the description of Death (pp. 57–58). Do the children find him comical, frightening or both? Discuss how Death helps the woman become rich and ask the children to speculate about what he might do in the next chapter, particularly how he might trick her.

Next steps
Refer to Activity Sheet 4: "Death, the Trickster?", in which the children are asked to write a character study of Death and how he might try to outwit the woman.

Death, the Trickster?

What is Death like in the story? Write a character study of him. Think about:

- what he looks like
- how he helps the woman
- how he claims his victims.

Add a final paragraph saying how you think he might trick the woman.

Death was not the most handsome of creatures. In fact he was…

_____

_____

_____

_____

_____

_____

_____

_____

_____

_____

_____

_____

_____

_____

_____

_____

White Wolves Teachers' Resource
for Guided Reading Year 5
Stories from Different Cultures
© A & C Black 2009

Ever Clever Eva: Teaching Sequence 5

Summary of Chapter Five

When the woman arrives at the palace, Death has placed himself at the foot of the bed. Quickly, the woman turns the bed around and the prince wakes up. They marry, there is a great feast and they ride away. However, Death is waiting. He kidnaps the woman and takes her to a room where millions of oil lamps are lit. Each represents a life. The woman's lamp is so low that she will soon die. So she asks Death if she can tell him a story. Death falls asleep and the woman quickly fills her lamp and the prince's and escapes. By this time, the judge is fast asleep. Eva calls the servants to take him up to bed and then they carry him to her father's cottage. The judge wakes, and Eva tells him that she has done what he asked. She has left taking the thing dearest to her – himself. The judge laughs, forgives the quick-witted Eva and makes her judge of the town in his place.

Teaching Sequence

Introduction
Recap on Chapter Four and ask the children to sum up what has happened to Eva so far, in a few sentences.

Independent reading
Ask the children to read Chapter Five. Emphasise reading for meaning.

- Discuss the meaning of unfamiliar or difficult words and phrases: *dabbed, marble* (p. 67), *four-poster bed, fashioned, despair, inspiration, shooting star* (p. 68), *glint* (p. 69), *whipped, Milky Way, oil lamps, universe* (p. 70), *IMMORTAL, despair* (p. 71), *confused* (p. 76).
- How quickly can the children find the similes on pp. 68, 69, 71, 73, 76 and 77?

Returning to the text
Build on children's understanding by asking questions during reading or when the chapter is finished. Encourage them to point to evidence in the story to support their answers.

1) What trick does the woman play on Death? (She turns the bed around so Death is at its head and the prince is cured (p. 68).)
2) What are Death's oil lamps? (They represent the lives of all the people in the universe (p. 70).)
3) How does the woman escape Death? (She tells him a story and he falls asleep (pp. 71–73).)
4) Why do you think Eva's husband forgives her? (She convinces him that he is the thing dearest to her and he is impressed by her wisdom (p. 77).)

Reread p. 72 and ask the children: What story does the woman begin to tell Death? Where have you heard it before? Elicit from the children that it is Eva's story within the second story, and it takes us back to the beginning of *Ever Clever Eva*.

Ask the children to work in pairs to explore these questions: How does Eva use a story to change her husband's mind? How does the woman escape from Death by telling a story? Call the pairs together and discuss how the story genre in *Eva Clever Eva* is like a bedtime tale: comforting, encourages sleep, casts a spell.

Discuss the ending of the tale, "lived cleverly everly after", and how it plays with the traditional folk-tale ending, twisting it to show how Eva's cleverness triumphs. Explore how using one's wits is critical to many folk and fairy tales, such as *Hansel and Gretel*. The children can suggest others.

Next steps
Refer to Activity Sheet 5: "Two Tales", in which the children separate the events in the two stories as told in the last chapter.

Two Tales

Draw up two lists about what happens in the last chapter. The first should list what happens to the woman and Death. The second should describe what happens to Eva and the judge.

The woman and Death	Eva and the judge
• The woman visits the prince and cures him by turning his bed around cheating death.	• The judge thinks the story is clever and begins to feel sleepy.
• The woman marries the prince.	• _____
• _____	• _____
• _____	• _____
• _____	• _____
• _____	• _____
• _____	• _____

White Wolves Teachers' Resource
for Guided Reading Year 5
Stories from Different Cultures
© A & C Black 2009

Bamba Beach by *Pratima Mitchell*

About the book

Hari lives with his parents and sister, Radha, in a small village in Goa. His father, a fisherman, cannot make a living without a modern fishing boat, which he cannot afford. So Hari, a clever and versatile boy, is constantly thinking of ways to make money, often at night when he can't sleep. Next door lives Madhu, with his wife, his three quarrelsome daughters, Tara, Anjali and Seema, his frail mother, Amma, and Motu the cat. There is no love lost between Madhu's family, (the "Next Doors") and Hari's ("Them Over There") and there is considerable jealousy in the village, since Amma has given her son his inheritance early. This has allowed Madhu to become a successful fisherman with a modern boat. But when Motu disappears and Hari finds him, the boy becomes the girls' hero and relations between the families begin to thaw.

As family debts grow, Hari is increasingly desperate to make money and takes on a car-washing job, given to him by his head teacher, Brother Angelo. He also discovers that Anjali, though bright, cannot write well and he offers to help her. Friendship between the children develops. Soon Hari's car washing expands, but money is still short and one night, when he is once more plotting what to do, a shadow flits past his window and he decides to follow. He finds Amma at the sea shore behaving strangely. Worried, Hari follows her to the creek, where he rescues her from a dangerous quicksand. Hailed as a hero, Brother Angelo grants Hari a scholarship to pay his school fees, while Amma gives him a valuable gold necklace as a reward, and for his kindness to Anjali and Motu. Now Hari's family can open a shop and with the profits buy a new boat. The story ends as Amma, Hari and the girls, now all good neighbours, take a walk along the beach.

in her cupped hands and lifting them above her head. She opened her fingers, letting the water splash over her face and head. Hari thought she might be praying to the ocean. Or maybe she was doing a spell. Her actions were slow and regular.

Amma turned round, so Hari hid himself as best he could by sitting down behind a big rock. The old lady stumbled about in the wet sand, peering here and there, as though she was looking for something. She picked up a piece of driftwood and flung it into the waves. She gazed out to sea.

64

Chapter Five

65

Bamba Beach: Teaching Sequence 1

Summary of Chapter One

Hari is unable to sleep and hears his parents discussing their money problems. A shadow flits past his window. Is it the Witch from next door? Next morning his father reminds him that neither Hari nor his sister Radha must associate with the "Next Doors", though Hari is uncertain why. Hari and Radha run down to the beach, where Hari meets some tourists. Encouraged at the possibility of earning some rupees, he offers to take them for a trip round the bay. They refuse, and Hari is left wondering how he can make some money.

Teaching Sequence

Introduction
Discuss the front cover and read the blurb. Find Goa on a world map and explain that it is part of India.

Independent reading
Ask the children to read Chapter One. Emphasise reading for meaning.

- Discuss the meaning of unfamiliar or difficult words, names and phrases: *wiry, harvest, rupees* (p. 7), *sprat, pomfret, kingfish, lobster, Konkani, Man in the Moon* (p. 8), *nibbling, bluebottles, squid, tentacles, shoals, sprat, plankton, Milky Way* (p. 9), *horizon, eavesdrop, tsunami* (p. 10), *physically affected, ocean currents steel-hulled, outboard motor* (p. 11), *compound, fisherfolk, cackle* (p. 12), *Lord Krishna, black magic* (p. 13), *dollars, roubles* (p. 14), *creek, scuttling, squabble* (p. 15), *seldom* (p. 17), *President, possibilities* (p. 18).
- Refer to the humour of the idiom, "Hari wasn't one to blow his own conch shell" (p. 7). Discuss the euphemism used for the neighbours, the "Next Doors" (p. 12) and the prejudice, "the Witch" (p. 12) and what they tell us about the relationship with the neighbours.

Returning to the text
Build on children's understanding by asking questions during reading or when the chapter is finished. Encourage them to point to evidence in the story to support their answers.
1) What do we find out about Hari straightaway? (His list of accomplishments give a vivid picture of him and create humour (pp. 7–8).)
2) Why do you think Hari's family and the villagers dislike Hari's neighbours? Discuss how gossip may be rooted in jealousy.

Refer to the way the author evokes the story's Indian setting from the outset. Discuss where Hari lives in Goa ("many miles from the nearest town"), the language he speaks ("Konkani"), the climate ("One hot November night") and the references to religion. Ask the children if they can find other references that give clues to the story's setting.

In this chapter we have a strong impression of the coastal setting at night. Discuss the use of languid images, "ink-black shadows", "waves curling in and out" (p. 9) and sometimes alliteration, "line of silvery surf" (p. 9) or personification, "the coconut palms rustled their underskirts" (p. 11). Discuss how these images link to Hari's sleepy mood.

Discuss the character of Hari, asking the children if they would like him for a friend and if so, why? Refer to his character traits, for example, he is imaginative (he conjures up images of sea creatures (p. 9)), resourceful (he thinks of ways of making money (p. 17)), optimistic (p. 18). Ask the children to offer their own words to describe Hari.

Next steps
Refer to Activity Sheet 1: "A Job for Hari?", ensuring the children understand what a reference is. Remind them that they must say what Hari would be like at the job and can refer to relevant events in the chapter.

A Job for Hari?

Imagine Hari is offered a job in a tea shop and you are asked to write a reference (a report) about him. The qualities needed for the job are listed below. Write Hari's reference in a polite, formal way. Take what we know about Hari into account and say why you think he would be good at the job or not.

Qualities needed for the job:
- honesty
- reliability
- ability to work hard
- practicality
- good at arithmetic
- good at reading and writing
- have a sense of humour

Dear Sir,

Thank you for your letter. I am pleased to send the reference you requested for Hari.

    First of all, let me say that he _____

_____

_____

_____

_____

_____

_____

_____

_____

_____

White Wolves Teachers' Resource
for Guided Reading Year 5
Stories from Different Cultures
© A & C Black 2009

Bamba Beach: Teaching Sequence 2

Summary of Chapter Two

Amma ("the Witch") lives with her son, Madhu, his wife and three daughters, Tara, Anjali and Seema. Amma has given Madhu his inheritance before she dies, enabling him to become a successful fisherman, but evoking jealousy in the community. We learn that Anjali is creative but has difficulties with her school work and that Seema would like to play with Radha. Seema tells her troubles to the family cat, Motu, but then Motu disappears. When Hari rescues Motu from a coconut palm, he becomes the sisters' hero, and the frosty relations between the two families thaw.

Teaching Sequence

Introduction
Recap on the characters in Hari's family and ask the children what Hari is concerned about and what he is determined to do.

Independent reading
Ask the children to read Chapter Two. Emphasise reading for meaning.

- Discuss the meaning of unfamiliar or difficult words and phrases: *vague, inheritance* (p. 21), *trade, dowry* (p. 22), *go-ahead* (p. 23), *goblins, sundown, ritual* (p. 24), *groomed, plaited* (p. 25), *great-grandfather, generations* (p. 26), *sleekest,* (p. 27), *trespass, reassuringly, morsels, king of the castle* (p. 28), *haunts* (p. 29).
- Ask the children if they know the game Knuckles (p. 27). (It is an ancient game played with stones or shells, sometimes called "Jacks".)

Returning to the text
Build on children's understanding by asking questions during reading or when the chapter is finished. Encourage them to point to evidence in the story to support their answers.
1) In what way is the picture of Amma different from that presented in Chapter One? (She is generous to her son, tolerant of her daughter-in-law, kind to her granddaughters (pp. 21–23).)
2) How do the family react when Motu is lost? (They are very concerned. Seema thinks he's dead (pp. 28–30).)
3) Why is Hari a "hero"? What other words could describe him? (For example, good-natured, thoughtful and, in particular, neighbourly.)

Discuss the character of Amma. Is it fair that she is called "the Witch"? Why have people "stopped speaking to her" (p. 21)? Do you think she was right to give her son his inheritance early?

Point out Amma's remark about the tourists (p. 25) What does she mean? You may also wish to refer back to Chapter One and discuss Hari's experience with the tourists (p. 17) and expand the discussion to consider issues outside the story. (For example, the Western companies that run the resorts in Goa retain the profits from tourism. The local economy does not benefit much.)

Discuss the role of girls in Indian society. Refer to Madhu's comment about pulling Anjali out of school and making her help her mother instead and also his comment: "Don't you know that girls have to go out to work these days?" (p. 24). Discuss why a dowry is important and why Amma is happy to have only daughters for grandchildren.

Draw attention to the way the author brings the chapter to a close. The repetition of the word "something" in the last lines emphasises the change in attitudes. It also makes the reader want to read on.

Next steps
Refer to Activity Sheet 2: "A Way of Life", in which the childre must write about the setting and culture depicted in Chapters One and Two.

A Way of Life

Write what you have learned about where the story is set and the characters' way of life. Write a paragraph for each of the following points, supporting your summaries with examples from the text:

- where the village is located and why tourists visit

_____

_____

_____

_____

- the climate, plants and insects

_____

_____

_____

_____

- the jobs the adults do and why some children work

_____

_____

_____

_____

- the traditions and customs and how life is changing

_____

_____

_____

_____

White Wolves Teachers' Resource
for Guided Reading Year 5
Stories from Different Cultures
© A & C Black 2009

Bamba Beach: Teaching Sequence 3

Summary of Chapter Three

Hari's parents are short of food. Hari and Radha visit the grocer to get rice on credit, and the miserly grocer reluctantly agrees. In a desperate effort to support his family, Hari seeks work from Brother Angelo, his head teacher, who gives Hari a job cleaning his car and also tells him that he and Radha can have free milk. Welcome though this is, it will not solve the family's problems and Hari daydreams about owning a little shop. In the meantime, Amma is wandering along the beach at night, staring at the waves and muttering to herself.

Teaching Sequence

Introduction
Ask the children to summarise the events in Chapters One and Two and list the main characters that have been introduced.

Independent reading
Ask the children to read Chapter Three. Emphasise reading for meaning.

- Discuss the meaning of unfamiliar or difficult words and phrases: *on credit, fretting, labourer* (p. 35), *dal* (p. 36), *forage, Bollywood film, State Bank of India* (p. 37), *maggoty, liquor* (p. 38), *detergent* (p. 39), *despair, determination, beeline* (p. 40), *drastic, colony, Portugal, Goans, Hindu* (p. 41), *hopscotch* (p. 43), *papaya* (p. 44).
- Point to the simile in the final lines of the chapter, "as light as a small scoop of sand" (p. 45), and why it suits Amma.

Returning to the text
Build on children's understanding by asking questions during reading or when the chapter is finished. Encourage them to point to evidence in the story to support their answers.

1) Why is Hari's father's new job insufficient to keep the family? (He is poorly paid. Explain how he is caught up in a cycle of debt: he cannot pay off his debts and has to borrow further, acquiring more debt.)
2) Why do Hari and Radha visit the grocer and how are they made to feel? (Hari and Radha are sent to get rice on credit and are humiliated by the shopkeeper when they ask (pp. 37–38).)
3) Why is Hari so unsympathetic to Radha's comments when they return from the shop? (He is worried about the family's circumstances and impatient with her impractical suggestion.)

Ensure the children grasp how the grocer became rich through lending money (p. 36).

Discuss the history of Bamba beach and Goa as a Portuguese colony and the subsequent religious mix of the village (p. 41). Point out that we can often learn interesting facts from fiction set in different cultures and historical times.

Draw attention to the phrase, "the waves lit by the strange magical gleam of phosphorus" (p. 45). Link this to Hari's dreamy state and to the earlier description of the sea at night discussed in Chapter One. Remind the children that the author creates links between the slow rhythm of the waves and the rhythm of dreams. Ask the children to create their own images linking the sea with dreams.

Ask the children what daydreaming is. (Wishes or hopes that may never be fulfilled.) Explore why Hari daydreams about owning a shop. Does it help him cope with the worries that he has? Contrast Hari's daydream with his daily life, ensuring the children grasp how far apart they are.

Next steps
Refer to Activity Sheet 3: "Hari's Daydream", which asks them to write two contrasting diary entries. The first should depict the reality of Hari's life, the second should depict his daydream.

Hari's Daydream

Imagine you are Hari. Write two diary entries for the same day.

The first should be an account of your day in Chapter Three, and the ups and downs you experience. Reread the chapter and decide what to include. Remember how worried you are about your family.

The second should be written as though your daydream of owning a shop is true. Describe what is on the shelves and how you have had a successful day selling your goods to different customers.

Remember to write in the first person, "I", as though you are Hari.

First diary entry

_____

_____

_____

_____

_____

Second diary entry

_____

_____

_____

_____

_____

White Wolves Teachers' Resource
for Guided Reading Year 5
Stories from Different Cultures
© A & C Black 2009

Bamba Beach: Teaching Sequence 4

Summary of Chapter Four

A fight develops between the girls next door and Seema runs in search of Motu for comfort. But Motu prefers it next door. So Seema talks to Hari. Tara discovers what Seema has been doing and another quarrel begins. This time it is Anjali who goes in search of Motu, and again it is Hari who listens and offers to help with her writing. Word spreads that Hari is washing cars and soon he has several customers. He continues to help Anjali, whose work improves. A few weeks later, Hari wakes to see a shadow heading for the beach. He follows and discovers it is Amma.

Teaching Sequence

Introduction

Recap on the events of Chapter Three, asking the children to describe the situation of Hari's family.

Independent reading

Ask the children to read Chapter Four. Emphasise reading for meaning.

- Discuss the meaning of unfamiliar or difficult words and phrases: *exhausted, veranda* (p. 50), *interfere, rebuffed, to-do, protested, lordly* (p. 51), *parish, hesitated, commotion* (p. 52), *guava tree, Margao* (p. 53), *high tide* (p. 54), *piped up* (p. 56), *Fernando* (p. 58), *contract, calculated* (p. 59), *monsoon* (p. 60), *suspiciously* (p. 62), *nimbly, eddied* (p. 63), *driftwood* (p. 64).
- Ask the children to find the simile describing the sisters' squabbles: "like knitting a very long scarf…" (p. 49).
- Discuss the powerful verbs used at the end of the chapter: *swirled, eddied* (p. 63), *stumbled, peering, flung* (p. 64).

Returning to the text

Build on children's understanding by asking questions during reading or when the chapter is finished. Encourage them to point to evidence in the story to support their answers.

1) How can we tell that the sisters have a comfortable life compared to Hari and Radha? (Motu is fed good food (p. 50), Madhu's fishing business is doing well (p. 54).)
2) Why is Anjali upset and why do you think she tells Hari and Radha? (She has difficulty with her work, and she is so unhappy that has to share it with someone (p. 56).)
3) In what way is Hari's job a success, but still not good enough? (He gets more car-washing work, but he calculates that it would take 15 years to make enough to buy a shop (pp. 58–60).)

In pairs, children can carry out a role play as Hari and Anjali, in which they discuss her difficulties with writing. Allow the children a few minutes to reread pp. 56–57.

Ask the children to consider in what way Amma is the wisest adult. (Madhu suspects Hari's motive for helping Anjali, while Amma understands that Hari "had a good heart" (p. 62).) Contrast this with Amma's nightly wanderings, which arouse Hari's concern (pp. 63–64). Refer back to the discussion of Amma in Lesson Two and encourage the children to recognise that Amma is a complex character.

Discuss the ways Motu brings the families together. Refer back to Chapter Two, when Motu becomes lost and is rescued by Hari (p. 31). Then refer to his behaviour in this chapter (pp. 51–53) and elicit from the children the train of events he unwittingly instigates.

Next steps

Refer to Activity Sheet 4: "Motu's Thoughts". Ask the children what the families might learn from him. Though he shows no loyalty to his family, he does treat both families equally.

Motu's Thoughts

Imagine you are Motu. Describe what he might be thinking.
Consider:

- what kinds of things he likes
- how he is treated
- what he thinks about the two families
- why he is important in the story.

I am a beautiful, clever cat. Everyone thinks so. I have a sleek, black coat and

like to eat dainty morsels of...

_____

_____

_____

_____

_____

_____

_____

_____

_____

_____

_____

_____

White Wolves Teachers' Resource
for Guided Reading Year 5
Stories from Different Cultures
© A & C Black 2009

Bamba Beach: Teaching Sequence 5

Summary of Chapter Five

Hari is worried about Amma and follows her towards the creek. When she becomes caught in quicksand he rescues her with a bamboo pole. Soon the whole neighbourhood is congratulating Hari the hero and Brother Angelo grants him a scholarship. The neighbours also reward him with sweets and a special gift brought by Motu – a valuable gold necklace. With the money the necklace will bring, Hari's family can open a shop, and with the profits buy a new boat.

Teaching Sequence

Introduction
Recap on the previous four chapters, asking the children to recall the main events. How do they think the story will end?

Independent reading
Ask the children to read Chapter Five. Emphasise reading for meaning.

- Discuss the meaning of unfamiliar or difficult words and phrases: *debris* (p. 67), *sari, curious, brushwood, hermit crab* (p. 68), *shallow, quicksand, thrashing* (p. 69), *bamboo pole* (p. 70), *bush telegraph* (p. 72), *dyslexia, scholarships* (p. 73), *jalebi, barfi* (p. 74), *medallions* (p. 75), *spick and span* (p. 76), *dinghy* (p. 77), *prim and proper* (p. 78).
- Ask the children to find the verb and simile describing Amma: "scuttled along like a hermit crab..." (p. 68) and the quicksand: "The mud was as thick as treacle" (p. 70).

Returning to the text
Build on children's understanding by asking questions during reading or when the chapter is finished. Encourage them to point to evidence in the story to support their answers.

1) How does Hari's good sense save Amma? (He knows he will be pulled into the quicksand if he offers his hand, so he returns for the bamboo pole (pp. 72–73).)
2) What happens to Hari when he arrives at school? (The children congratulate him, he is rewarded by Brother Angelo for his bravery and also kindness to Anjali (pp. 72–73).)
3) Why do you think Motu is chosen to deliver the necklace? (Motu first bridged the gap between the neighbours.)

Discuss the themes in the story: friendship / neighbourliness, prejudice, sibling rivalry, being poor, age / wisdom. The children can work in pairs to decide what they think the main theme in the story is. To help, they could ask themselves what overall impression they are left with at the end. Also refer back to Lesson One and the work done by the children about Hari's character. All the qualities he has shown in the story combine to bring about a positive change in his own and others' lives. Remind the children that Hari is described as a hero. What do they think a "hero" is? Ask them to check in a dictionary and discuss various definitions. In what way is Hari a hero? (For example, he is the principal character in the story, and someone who is brave and laudable.)

Point to the way in which the story ends, with a walk along the seashore. Discuss why this is particularly fitting, noting that several of the chapters finish on the beach or with a reference to the sea. The children could discuss in groups in what ways the sea is a motif in the story. (For example, the families are fisherman and depend on the sea for their living, the sea has a soothing effect, but is also dangerous and powerful, particularly when Amma is drawn to it).

Next steps
Refer to Activity Sheet 5: "It Could Have Been So Different...", in which the children write an alternative ending to the story.

It Could Have Been So Different...

Many good things came to Hari because of his actions, but it could have been so different if he hadn't followed Amma. Write an alternative ending to the story thinking about:

- what might have happened to Amma
- how Hari would have felt if he had chosen not to help her
- how Amma's family would have felt
- what might have happened to Hari's family without money.

White Wolves Teachers' Resource
for Guided Reading Year 5
Stories from Different Cultures
© A & C Black 2009

Record Card

Group: **Book:**

Focus for Session:

Names	Comments

Record Card

The White Wolves Interview:
Patrice Lawrence

Patrice Lawrence is Sussex-born, Hackney-living, from a Caribbean and Italian family. Patrice has always written – poetry until her teens, short stories in her twenties, screenplays in her thirties, and now a mash-up of all of it. Her secret ambition is to write a horror story.

Where did you get your ideas from for *Granny Ting Ting*?

I steal ideas from my family! My mother has never managed to ride a bike, in spite of having a good try. She still has the scars to prove it. "Granny" is based on an aunty. And my daughter is a tomboy who won't let boys beat her at anything.

What do you like best about the finished story?

It's great when all the ideas, pictures and silent conversations swirling around in your head finally shape themselves into the story you want to tell.

How long does it take to write a story and do you redraft it?

The title usually comes first and then the story idea follows quite quickly. But then there's lots and lots of rewriting and redrafting to make sure that it all makes sense and characters don't change name and hair colour halfway through.

Do you have a special place where you write, or can you write anywhere?

My bags and drawers are full of scribbled-on paper from train journeys, bus journeys and boring meetings. But I do most of the computery stuff in a bedroom in East London.

How old were you when you started writing? What were your early stories like?

I started writing poems when I was about seven or eight, and probably stories, too. When I was 11, I composed bedtime stories for my little brother, Lee, about a giant purple rabbit called Chigawig who flew him on a giant carrot over a rainbow to hunt cheeses. I'm surprised he didn't have nightmares.

What other writers do you particularly admire?

I love writers who can make different worlds real – Philip Reeve, Philip Pullman, Philip K. Dick. I like authors not called "Philip" too, though.

The White Wolves Interview: Andrew Fusek Peters

Andrew Fusek Peters has written over 70 books for children. When he isn't stuck behind his computer, you can find him doing author visits all over the country with his didgeridoo, juggling balls and skateboard.

His latest books include the thrilling new series *Skateboard Detectives*. For A&C Black he has written *The Story Thief* and *Ever Clever Eva*. You can find out more about him and his work at www.tallpoet.com

Do you enjoy folk tales? What do you think they can teach us?

Yes. They can give us a more subtle, imaginative way of thinking and, particularly with these folk tales, that there is always a solution to every problem – you just have to use your brain!

Where do you get your ideas from?

These two stories are traditional – the first one was passed on by my mother and she grew up knowing the tale. The death story came from a book of Czech tales and I have adapted it freely!

What ingredients do you think a good story should have?

Lots of good twists, unexpected events, a strong narrative and characters who win through in the end.

How do you know a story is working? Do you ever abandon a story and start something else?

When working with traditional stories, you want to make sure that your retelling is sparky, well written and adding a fresh angle to an old story. With novels, the same rules apply except that you are looking for the flow, for the question of what happens next and that the reader really wants to know. I have abandoned novels and had several unpublished novels that now, looking back, I can see didn't work properly. It takes a long time to learn how to build a well crafted story.

What stories did you enjoy when you were a child?

I loved *The Hobbit*, *The Lord of the Rings*, horror and World War II commando comics (i.e. stories with pictures), Enid Blyton (I admit it!) and lots of science fiction (Asimov, etc.).

In what way is writing a story different from writing a poem?

You have a larger canvas with which to play and more time to express what's inside you. Nothing beats creating a whole world, filling it with characters and setting them on a path.

The White Wolves Interview:
Pratima Mitchell

Pratima Mitchell loves her bike, swimming, growing flowers and vegetables, reading and going on long journeys. Pratima travels a lot and is often in India, exploring her heritage. She is learning the melodeum (a small, accordian-type instrument) and is interested in just about everything.

Her new book for teens, *Indian Summer*, will be published in 2009 and she is working on a thriller set in France and India. She lives in Oxford, where her desk overlooks the Thames, and swans gliding past.

What sparked the idea for *Bamba Beach*?

I once lived next door to a family of three girls on a lovely beach in Goa. I can still picture the sights and sounds of the beach and the old "witch" who was the girls' granny. Everyone in the village was afraid of her.

Does your own childhood play a part in any of your stories?

There isn't a writer in the world whose childhood – and life story – isn't the flavour of the juice he / she squeezes from their imagination. The short answer to my convoluted sentence is "yes"!

Do you have a plan before you begin writing, and do you know how your story will end?

I start with the sound of a "ping" in my head. This miraculously becomes a taste, a smell, a picture of a place and finally a sentence. That sentence leads to another, and another and another … and hey, the story is written! I usually let the characters decide what they want to happen.

What is your writing day like?

I work hard in the mornings, from nine to lunch and party the rest of the day in my allotment.

Have any other writers influenced your own writing?

I admire Jane Gardam, Ann Tyler, Philip Pullman, Charles Dickens, Cormac McCarthy, Rose Tremain, Chekov, Tolstoy … far too many to list!

Do you think your stories should carry a message as well as entertain?

A good story always has a hidden message, straight from the soul of the writer.

White Wolves Resources for Guided Reading

Year 3

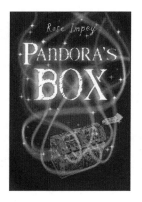

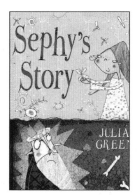

White Wolves Resources for Guided Reading

Year 4

Stories about Imagined Worlds, Science-Fiction and Fantasy
ANN WEBLEY
Teachers' Resource for Guided Reading

Stories That Raise Issues
KARINA LAW
Teachers' Resource for Guided Reading

Stories from Different Cultures
KARINA LAW
Teachers' Resource for Guided Reading

Stories with Historical Settings
KARINA LAW
Teachers' Resource for Guided Reading

Hugo and the Long Red Arm
Rachel Anderson

Julia Green
Taking Flight

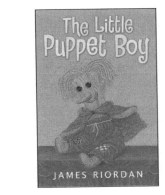

The Little Puppet Boy
JAMES RIORDAN

THE QUEEN'S TOKEN
Pamela Oldfield

JENNY OLDFIELD
Live the Dream

J. Alexander
FINDING FIZZ

The Story Thief
Andrew Fusek Peters

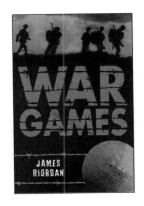

WAR GAMES
JAMES RIORDAN

DIANA HENDRY
SWAN BOY

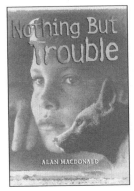

Nothing But Trouble
ALAN MACDONALD

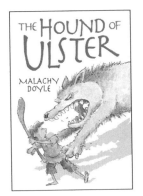

THE HOUND OF ULSTER
MALACHY DOYLE

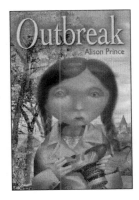

Outbreak
Alison Prince

White Wolves Resources for Guided Reading

Year 5

Year 6

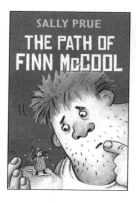

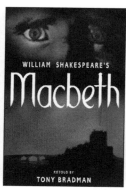

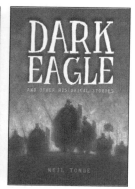

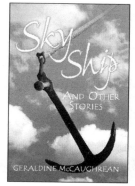

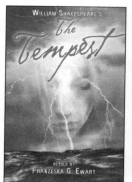

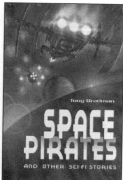